African Proverbs, Parables and Wise Sayings

SIERRA LEONE
WEST AFRICA

by
EYAMIDÉ ELLA LEWIS-COKER

Illustrated
by
Mrs. Eyamidé E. Lewis-Coker, MBA

authorHOUSE®

AuthorHouse™
1663 Liberty Drive
Bloomington, IN 47403
www.authorhouse.com
Phone: 1-800-839-8640

First published by AuthorHouse 5/2/2011

ISBN: 978-1-4520-1292-6 (sc)
ISBN: 978-1-4634-0207-5 (e)

Library of Congress Control Number: 2011903639

Printed in the United States of America

This book is printed on acid-free paper.

Dedication

To my wonderful, lovely husband:
Thank you for your constant encouragement and patience
in supporting me to write this book. I love you!

To my gorgeous, lovely children, Adetungie and Adeyemie Wills:
Thank you for your continuous support and encouragement
in assisting me to write and publish this book. You are my
inspiration and the absolute lights of my life. I love both of you!

To my lovely parents and grandparents:
Thank you for placing books in my hands at an early age and
never doubted that I could make it as a writer. I once called you
my very first editors, because you edited me into the person I
am today. You will always be in my heart. I love all of you!

To the citizens and friends of Sierra Leone:
You have inspired me to write this book. I hold all of
you close to my heart. Thanks and I love you all!

About the Author

Mrs. Eyamidé E. Lewis-Coker

Mrs. Eyamidé E. Lewis-Coker is from Sierra Leone, West Africa. She is a computer science lecturer at Wilshire Computer College and a Career Technical Education certificated project leader at Bassett Unified School District in Southern California.

She was a business lecturer at the Milton Margai Teachers' Training College and the University of Sierra Leone Institute of Public Administration and Management in Freetown, Sierra Leone, West Africa.

Proverbs, parables, and wise sayings serve as analogy that helps Africans to understand the significance of a message being communicated.

Mrs. Eyamidé E. Lewis-Coker has over forty years of expertise in writing West African proverbs, parables, and wise sayings. She holds a Masters degree in Business Administration and Management, and is currently living with her family in Southern California.

She contributes to several African magazines and presents regularly at major African cultural shows and events. She shares her knowledge during discussions and conversations using African words of wisdom to mention and convey the truth in an easily understandable way. She utilizes these words to point out where others have failed and to help others avoid the same mistakes. She also uses them to describe actions and to show results, morals, dilemmas, and consequences of choices made by people in their daily lives.

These ancestral proverbs, parables, and wise sayings are the essential vehicles that transmit African wisdom, morals, traditions, and values.

African Proverbs, Parables, and Wise
Sayings are the Experiences of Life

Acknowledgments

I would like to express my gratitude to all those who gave me the incentive to write this book, *African Proverbs, Parables, and Wise Sayings.*

A special thanks to those who provided support, discussed things over, read, wrote, offered comments, and assisted me in editing, proofreading, and designing this book.

I am deeply indebted to some of my departed family: my grandfather, grandmother, father, mother, uncles and aunts. Many thanks for their constant encouragement in enabling me to publish this book. Above all, I want to say special thanks to my husband, sons, grandchildren and siblings for supporting and encouraging me in spite of all the time it took me away from them. It was a long and difficult journey!

Last but not least, I would like to express thanks and appreciation to the rest of my family. I've not forgotten the brothers and sisters of Sierra Leone for their contributions in the process of selecting and editing this book.

Introduction

African proverbs, parables, and wise sayings express the wisdom of Africans, and are the tools utilized to understand the African people's past and present lives, This ancient African wisdom is the vehicle that transmits the African customs, morals, traditions, and values orally from generation to generation.

SIERRA LEONE

In Sierra Leone each ethnic group uses proverbs, parables, and wise sayings through everyday life.

The role and importance of the ancient African words of wisdom in each ethnic group's conversations provide a colorful and poetic picture of the culture and its characteristics.

Most proverbs, parables, and wise sayings are passed down by older men and women of each ethnic group, and these are guides that instruct each member of the group.

In conversations, they are used to illuminate the pitfalls and stumbling blocks along the road of life, pointing out where others have failed and helping others to avoid the same mistakes.

Each ethnic group utilizes ancient African wisdom in different ways. In some cases old people use it to chastise the young, and sometimes the young people use it to justify their actions.

There are times when African wisdom is used to give warnings to husbands on how to live and rule their household.

In many ways, proverbs, parables, and wise sayings are used in modes that one cannot always express in normal conversations. There are times when normal words cannot be expressed in ways you would like someone to understand them. In these cases you would use proverbs, parables, and wise sayings: "The daughters of experience!"

Sierra Leoneans utilize the ancient African wisdom as guiding lights or stepping stones to the next generation helping family members unite in their times of need, teaching wisdom and discipline to the young. Through this the young generation receives knowledge and purpose to do what is right, just and fair.

Proverbs, parables, and wise sayings do come in handy during conversations. In fact, without the use of the ancestral wisdom, the Creole culture would have lost much of its customs, morals, traditions, and values.

Contents

Accept the Fact, Acknowledge the Fact

-   What has been blown away by the wind will never be retrieved.

-   If a bowl of farina *"gari"* spills on pebbles, gravels, or rock fragments, what can you do?

Action, Performance, Manner, Deed, Activity

-   His hands are too short to box with God.

-   Knowledge is not the main thing, but deeds.

-   As you make your bed, so must you lie on it.

-   Ashes fly on the face of who throws the ashes.

-   No matter how old the cow is, his liver is not old.

-   He will certainly reap whatever he sows.

-   Whatever is planted will grow up.

-   He who has done good deeds will receive favor from above.

-   You must judge a man by the work of his hands.

-   He who has done evil will expect evil.

-   A good deed is something one returns.

-   You have seen today, but what about tomorrow?

-   He who expels saliva will not retract it.

-   Do good because of tomorrow.

-   He who lives by the sword will die by the sword.

-   If you climb up a tree, you must climb down the same tree.

- He who digs up a grave for his enemy may be digging it for himself.

Advantage, Selfish Profit

- Invite someone into your parlor, and he will certainly occupy your bedroom.

- It is your own grease that the con artist will use to fry you alive, if you are not careful.

- It is the rotten corpse that belongs to Jesus.

Advice, Counsel, Guidance

- When you fall into the path of your father, you learn to walk like him.

- A word for the wise is quite sufficient.

- It is a bad child who does not take advice.

Agree, Concur, Be Together, See Eye to Eye

- If you fall down for me, I will certainly fall down for you.

- His finger is just right for his friend's nostril.

- Two eyes are better than one.

Aggressive, Assertive, Pushy, Forceful, Rude

- He who asked questions will not avoid answers.

- An aggressor spat crushed kola nut in his mouth when he was born.

- When a turtle "*trukie*" grabs hold of something, it takes the noise of thunder to have it released.

- If you don't fight, you can't conquer.

- His tongue is sharper than steel.

- A baboon loves to holler; luckily a security guard's duty is assigned to a baboon.

- Even iron sharpens iron.

- It is iron that cuts iron.

Alike, Same, Similar

- A black cow also produces white milk.

- Monkey speaks; monkey understands.

- It is Mr. Old Man Monkey who marries Mrs. Old Woman Monkey.

- When it rains, the same rain that produces sweet sugar cane also produces bitter lemon leaves.

- He who drinks beer, thinks beer.

- Like father, like son.

- Like mother, like daughter.

- It takes a vulture to shave another a vulture.

Ambition, Aspiration, Desire, Dream, Goals

- A man with too much ambition will not sleep in peace.

- The elephant's head is not a load for a child.

- To try and fail is not laziness.

- Help yourself, and God will help you.

- It takes great people to make a great company.

- If you climb the ladder, you must start at the bottom.

- If you cease to dream, you will cease to live.

- If you want your eggs "*aigê*" to be hatched, you have to sit on the eggs "*aigê*."

- The want of a thing is good for something.

- Strive hard to accomplish your dreams.

- People with goals succeed because they know where they are going.

- A goal is a dream with a deadline.

Arrogant, Bigheaded, Conceited, Proud, Condescending

- Strive very hard to accomplish your dreams instead of bragging about your education.

Attach, Affix, Clip, Connect

- If you are the cup handle, beware of the cup.

Bad, Awful, Terrible, Evil, Wicked, Corrupt

- A bad workman quarrels with his tools.

- An evil eye sees no good.

- The first thing a bad trader offered for sale was his honesty.

- A bad neighbor lends a needle without a thread.

- A bad man may be under a good coat.

Beautiful, Attractive, Gorgeous, Good-Looking, Fine-Looking

- To try really hard to be beautiful does not hurt.

- Beauty is skin deep.

- Beauty is in the eyes of the beholder.

- A beautiful thing is not a perfect thing.

- All that glitters is not gold.

- Beauty without virtue is like a flower without perfume.

- Not all pretty apples are good.

- A pretty shoe may pinch the foot.

- A pretty woman does not need to try to be pretty.

- He who marries a beauty, marries trouble.

Believe, Accept As True

- Seeing is different from being told.

- Seeing is believing.

- Seeing is better than hearing.

- The proof is in the pudding.

- The proof of the porridge "*pap*" is worth the eating.

Brag, Boast, Show Off

- If your yams are white in color, conceal or cover them.

- Do not sing your own praises.

- Do not blow your own trumpet/horn.

- The ink is still not dry in your pen.

- He who boasts a lot does little.

- He who sings "*Alleluia*" is not necessarily holy.

- A poor man owns a pig's head "*hog aide*"; he hangs it on a fence to dry.

- A chattering "*talk talk*" bird builds no nest.

- A roaring lion kills no game.

- Words are more easily said than action.

- A meowing cat catches no mice.

- An empty pot makes the most noise.

- A person of words and no deed is like a garden full of weeds.

- Do not boast of being pretty; beauty is skin deep.

- Do not boast of being beautiful; beauty is from the beholder.

- Boasting continuously is not necessary.

Be Careful, Beware, Be Cautious, Think Twice, Watch Out, Take Heed

- Family tie is like a tree; it bends but never breaks.

- A hen with chicks does not jump a fire.

- When a dog bites his master, it will bite a stranger.

- If you do not step on a dog's tail, it will not bite you.

- A close friend can become your close enemy.

- Beware of a dog's tooth and a woman's tongue.

- If you make yourself a mouse, the cat will catch you.

- No one tests the depth of a river with both feet.

- A cow that has no tail should not try to chase flies.

- A cow that has no tail, God chases its flies.

- A cow has no business with horseplay.

- A fish that keeps his mouth shut will not be caught.

- If you notice a man dragging a rope, look out the rope is around a cow's neck.

- If a strong wind is tossing a mortar "*martar odoe*" in the air, why should a bamboo winnowing fan "*fanner*" be on the ground?

- A bird with a broken leg does not fly really high.

- Never insult a crocodile until you cross the river.

- Cross the river before you talk about the crocodile's mother.

- A fly that dances carelessly in front of a spider's web risks the wrath of the spider's teeth "*teet.*"

- He who is bitten by a snake fears a lizard "*kondo.*"

- He who is bitten by a snake fears an ant "*anch.*"

- If you are hiding, do not light a fire.

- One must talk little, and listen a great deal.

- It is better for your feet to slip than your tongue.

- If you watch your pot, your food will not burn.

- If you are the cup handle, beware of the cup.

- If you play with edged tools, you may be cut.

- You will never win if you try to fight a pig "*hog*" in the mud "*portor-portor.*"

- Bathe other people's children, but don't wash behind their ears.

- Be sure that the candle is lit before you throw away the match.

- If a blind man "*blen yai man*" says let's throw stones, he has stepped on one.

- Look before you leap.

- Don't think there is no crocodile just because the river is calm.

- The face of the river is beautiful, but it is not safe to sleep on it.

- Wait patiently until a wet leopard "*soak lepet*" is dried up; then you will realize that the leopard "*lepet*" is not a cat "*puss.*"

- Even the small leopard "*lepet*" is called a leopard "*lepet.*"

- Do not awake sleeping dogs.

- Don't dig your own grave.

- If you are not cautious when you are making your deals, a dog will eat your supper.

- Hint knows its master and "*kabarslot or frock,*" a long Creole traditional female African dress, knows its mistress.

- When you want to insult a deaf man, do not insult him around his child.

- John who is always the accuser should not visit a garden eggs' farm. "*jarkarto farm*".

- If you are not careful, your grace will become a bundle of grass.

Character, Quality, Nature, Personality

- Tell me whom you love, and I'll tell you who you are.

- You will say that your child is more beautiful than my child, but the outlook and conduct of both are similar.

- As you sell yourself, so the world will buy you.

- You possess not the skills and talents, but your attitude and outlook make you a great professional.

Character Assassination, Defamation

- If you damage the character of another, you will damage your own.

- Your character follows you wherever you go.

Cheat, Swindle, Defraud or Rip Off; Corruption, Bribery, Sleaze, Dishonesty

- A con artist buries a con artist.

- Where there is smoke, there is fire.

Concern, Interests

- Teeth do not mourn "*teet mor daé munin.*"

Conform, Obey the Rules

- A dog is an effective constable, but it will not patrol the street where the leopard "*lepet*" lives.

Contentment, Happiness, Satisfaction

- A rope is not appropriate for the fowl's neck "*fol neck,*" so it is tied on its feet.

- Being happy is better than being a king.

- A cow must graze where it is tied.

- An ugly man takes no notice of the mirror.

- It is better to go to heaven in rags than to hell in silk.

- A man that lives near the river will not use spit to wash his hands.

- A cow without a tail, God chases its flies.

- A half loaf of bread is better than none.

- Being poor and happy is better than being wealthy and miserable.

- One foot is better than two crutches.

- A bird in the hand is worth two in the bush.

- Do not drop the fish you have in your hand for the fish that touches your foot.

- However tightly packed a house might be, a hen finds a corner to lay eggs "*aigê*."

- A dog has four feet, but it does not travel four roads at once.

- When the door of happiness closes, another one opens.

Courage, Bravery

- You cannot cry over spilt milk.

- How much will you taste on ten-penny "*ten pence*" salt?

- You do not have to beat the baboon "*babu*" to death because of its ugliness.

- The baboon "*babu*" is extremely ugly, but he married the sister of the monkey.

- What has been blown away will not be retrieved.

- It takes shame to bite "*bet*" a caterpillar "*fatfut*."

- It takes embarrassment to bite "*bet*" a crab.

- You cannot throw water over a duck's back.

Courtesy, Good Manners, Politeness

- Courtesy costs nothing.

- A good tongue is a good weapon.

- A good word offers the best kola nut.

- A good word extinguishes more than fire.

- A good face needs no paint.

- A kind word is not wasted.

- He who is courteous is not a fool.

Coward

- A coward always hides behind someone else after he has thrown a stone.

- A dead cock "*dy kack*" never crows.

- A cat "*puss*" never cries where it is struck.

Criticize, Condemn, Pass Judgment on Someone

- Only when you have crossed the river, can you say the crocodile has a lump on his snout.

- If you try to clean others like soap, you will waste away in the process!

- Do not throw stones "*tone*" when you have glass windows.

- Foxes say the grapes are sour if they can't reach them.

- Do not point fingers when you have spotty glass windows.

- When your neighbor is wrong you point a finger, but when you are wrong you hide.

- Let not the pot call the kettle "*kittle*" black.

- Those who have glass windows should not throw stones.

- Let not the fermented sesame seeds, "*ogiri*" insult the fermented locust seeds, "*kendar*" for a typical smell.

11

- A bowl should not laugh when a calabash breaks.

- A camel never sees its own hump.

- A camel never sees the crookedness of its neck.

- Do not mend your neighbor's fence before checking on yours.

- Do not call the forest that shelters you a jungle.

- He who is unable to dance says that the yard is stony.

- If you have one finger pointing at somebody, you will have three pointing toward you.

- A monkey does not see his own hind part; he sees his neighbor.

- He who cannot dance will say the beat of the drum is awful.

- Before healing others, please heal thyself.

- Before you remove dirt from one's eyes, remove the dirt in your eye first.

- Glance at the image in the mirror before pointing fingers.

- A baboon laughs at the buttocks of another baboon.

- A monkey never thinks her baby is ugly.

- The mother-in-law does not remember that she was a daughter-in-law.

- The old cow thinks she was never a calf.

Danger, Risk, Jeopardy

- A fly that dances carelessly in front of a spider's web, risks the wrath of the spider's teeth "*teet.*"

- A fly has no business dancing in front of a lizard "*kondo.*"

- A bird "*bord*" with fire on its tail burns its own nest.

- A child "*pickin*" who is fearless is going to bring tears to his mother's "*mama*" eyes.

- A bird "*bord*" that prays for rain will find itself soaked.

- Do not step on the dog's tail, and it will not bite you.

- Don't kick a sleeping dog.

- The dog's bark is not might, but fright.

- A dog cannot eat a bone tied to a snake.

- When a frog "*uporlor*" is tied around your foot, expect a snake.

- Do not try to fight a lion if you are not one yourself.

- When a cock "*kack*" is drunk, he forgets about the hawk "*ack*."

- Eggs "*aigé*" have no business dancing with stones.

- Rats "*aratar*" do not dance in the cat's "*puss*" doorway.

- Do not walk through the lion's path.

- A cockroach "*kackroach*" that crawls carelessly into a palm oil "*pam-mine*" bottle, risks its life.

- When a cockroach "*kackroach*" says, "I want to dance!" Please call the cock and allow the cock "*kack*" to beat the drum.

- Never insult a crocodile until you cross the river.

- The most dangerous thing a man needs is a woman.

- Do not walk into a snake pit with your eyes closed.

- Cows have no business in horseplay.

- Don't think there are no crocodiles just because the river is calm.

- A snake at your feet, a stick in your hand!

- A fowl "*fol*" will not spare a cockroach "*kackroach*" that falls into its midst.

- Instruct a cockroach "*kackroach*" to summon a fowl "*fol.*"

- He escaped from a frying pan relationship and ended up in a fire.

- If you play with fire, you will get burned.

- Fire has no brother.

- When a frog "*uporlor*" continues to hop in the afternoon, it is chased by a snake.

- The jackass says the world is not level.

Death, Bereavement, Passing Away

- Death does not sound a trumpet.

- Death is a part of life. No one escapes its clutches.

- Death is like a robe that everyone has to wear.

- Always being in a hurry does not prevent death; neither does going slowly prevent living.

- When brothers and sisters fight to the death, a stranger inherits their father's estate.

- Sleep is death's cousin.

- Death is like a strong breeze in front of one's door.

- Do not eyeball the cemetery depressingly; it is destined.

- Death is the key that will open the miser's coffin.

Deceive, Trick, Betray, Cheat, Mislead, Lie

- A schoolmaster was once a schoolboy.

- When the cat "*puss*" is away, the mouse "*aratar*" will play.

- When the leopard "*lepet*" is away, his cubs are eaten.

- A friend to everybody is a friend to nobody.

- When the master is absent, the frogs "*uporlor*" hop in the house.

- A fisherman will never say that his fish is rotten.

- John's palm oil "*pam-mine*" spilled on John's rice "*ress.*"

- Trick is smoke.

- He is a green snake in green grass.

Depend, Rely, Count On

- Do not depend on the dead man's shoes "*dy-man sus*" when you do not know his size.

- Do not count the chickens before they are hatched.

- Don't try to put old heads on young shoulders.

Destine, Predestine, Predetermine

- A stream of water will not pass you by, if it is destined.

- Destiny is not a matter of chance; it is a matter of choice.

- What God has planted, you do not have to water.

- You cannot take away someone's luck.

- Each man meets his own destiny.

- Whatever the case may be, you will receive your destiny.

Differ, Disagree, Conflict

- Children of the same mother do not always see eye to eye.

- We can't see eye to eye.

- A big-foot man does not join a small-foot dance.

- Pumpkin is not a soup, but in some instance, a pumpkin is a soup.

- Cassavas have the same skin, but not all taste the same.

- The snake and the crab do not sleep in the same hole.

- The spider and the fly do not bargain.

- Fire and gunpowder do not sleep together.

- Two waterfalls do not hear each other.

- All monkeys do not climb on the same tree.

- Every door has its own key.

- The spider and the lizard "*kondo*" do not see eye to eye.

- Two long-nose individuals do not kiss.

- Hearts do not meet one another like roads.

- Two great talkers do not travel together very far.

- Pride and grace do not stay in one place.

- If you tell friends to live together, you are telling them to quarrel.

Dislike, Hate, Detest

- One man's junk is another man's treasure.

- One man's meat is another man's poison.

Disrespectful, Impolite, Bad-mannered

- A dog you don't feed will never heed your call.

- It is how you conduct yourself that determines whether you will be selected to prepare a pot of African cassava paste, "*fufu/foo-foo*" during an African feast or ceremony known as; "*Awujoh or Awujor*".

- If you lie on the floor, someone will walk over you.

- A child who tries to wear his father's pants will continue to adjust the waistline with a string.

- If you make yourself into a doormat, people will wipe their feet on you.

- Charlotte "*Shalat nor no yai*" always ignores the rolling of someone's eyes.

- The words from her mouth are sharper than a sword.

- If your mouth turns into a knife, it will cut off your lip.

Dissuade, Win Over

- Do not fall into a river and turn into a fish.

- If you fall into a river, you have to swim or take a bath.

Drift, Lose the Point

- It is the wandering dog that finds the old bone.

Enemy, Opponent, Rival

- A close friend can become your close enemy.

- An intelligent enemy is better than a stupid friend.

- I am not the one that killed your cat.

- A good enemy is better than a bad friend.

- Your enemy will make you wise.

- Man's greatest enemy is man.

- If your enemy is like a mouse, watch him like a lion.

Establish, Secure, Gain Control

- A determined hunter "*hunting man*" is never frightened in the jungle.

Evil, Immoral

- Evil enters like a needle and spreads like an oak tree.

Exaggerate, Overstate, Overstress

- Do not make mountains out of molehills.

Excess, Surplus, Over the Limit

- A bowl of palava/palaver sauce "*plassas*"surpasses a plate of cooked rice.

- A cup of water surpasses a bowl of flour.

Exclude, Eliminate, Be Exclusive Of

- My dad "*papa*" is not a butcher; why should I know about the cost of a pig "*hog*"?

- When Joki's wooden stall "*Joki bander*" was burning, I was not around. Why should I put out the fire?

Experience, Knowledge, Understanding

- Proverbs are the daughters of experience.

- Experience teaches fools.

- He who learns teaches.

- Experience is the best teacher because it is always on the job.

- Experience is the mother of invention.

- Experience is a great teacher.

- A bird knows when the leaves will shake from a tree before the wind blows.

- He, who cuts a piece of cloth in two pieces, should know how to sew the two pieces cloth together again into one piece.

- A man who knows the use of proverbs reconciles differences.

Extravagant, Over the Top, Wasteful

- Never hang your hat higher than you can reach.

- Cut your coat according to your shape.

- A penny saved is a penny gained.

- Never bite more than you can chew.

Fact, Truth, Reality, Actuality

- Business is business.

- Black is black.

- White is white.

- If the chicken's feather is white, it is white.

- Truth may be blamed, but not shamed.

Faith, Confidence, Trust, Reliance, Assurance, Belief

- When the door of happiness closes, another one opens.

- Cast your troubles *"wahalar"* on the Lord, and he will be up all night anyway.

- If God sends you on stony paths, he will give you strong shoes.

- Faith drives out fear, but smiles drives out a tear.

False Friend

- A false friend is like a shadow; he will only be with you when the sun is shining.

Familiar, Associate

- Only if you live with a person will you know a person.

- Evil knows where evil sleeps.

- Rats know the way of other rats.

- The pumpkin vine never produces watermelons.

- An orange tree never produces lime or lemon fruits.

- The foot knows where the shoe pinches.

- Come visit me and come live with me are entirely different.

- Familiarity breeds contempt and distance breeds respect.

Family Relatives

- Family tie *"fambul ty"* is like a tree; it can bend but it cannot break.

- If you are the cup handle, beware of the cup.

- In any case, blood is thicker than water.

- If relatives help each other, what evil can hurt them?

- Family tree "*fambul tik*," if possible, will bend but will never break.

- Family will quarrel "*set kartar- kartar*" but will still be a family.

Favor, Kindness, Support, Good Turn, Preference

- African ingredient, "*Lubĩ*," is no slave for okra soup "*okro soup*"; it is doing the soup a favor.

- It is better to sweep your house clean than to sweep the street.

- Charity begins at home.

- A good turn deserves another.

- A new broom sweeps clean, but an old broom knows the corners.

Feelings, Way of Thinking, Viewpoint

- Only a monkey understands a monkey.

- It is Mr. Old Man Monkey who marries Mrs. Old Woman Monkey.

Finance, Money, Backing, Funding

- If the palm of the hand itches, it signifies the coming of great luck.

- Cut your coat according to your cloth.

- Take care of the pennies, and the dollars or pounds will take care of themselves.

- When money speaks, truth stays silent.

Financially Embarrassed, Without Money

- One cannot take nut oil "*nat-ty*" to deep-fry a stone.

- A turtle "*trukie wan box é an short*" will love to be a boxer, but its hands are too short to box.

- All lizards "*kondo*" crawl with their bellies, but it is very difficult to detect the lizard with an upset belly.

Fool, Unwise on a Given Situation

- A fool and a stream of water will go the way they are diverted.

- A fool looks for dung where the cow never browsed.

- By the time the fool has learned the game, the players have disappeared.

- It is better to be silent like a fool than to talk like one.

- A fool may chance to put something into a wise man's head.

- If you've been fooled once it is excusable, but if it happens twice then you are a fool.

- When a fool is insulted, he thinks he has been praised.

- Only a fool will try to jump a fire.

- A fool speaks; a wise man listens.

- A fool will part with his money.

- Humans make mistakes; fools repeat them.

- A fool is thirsty in the midst of water.

- It is the fool's sheep that breaks loose twice.

- Do not give a sharp tool to a fool.

- When a fool is told a proverb, its meaning has to be explained to him.

- He who walks with fools is a fool.

- A man starts as a fool and becomes wise after experience.

- A fool never learns.

Forever, Perpetual, Ceaseless

- Travel here and travel there; the riverside stone *"watar sy tone"* is still in its position.

- The stone that the builders rejected is the very headstone of the corner.

Forget, Fail to Remember

- Absence makes the heart forget.

Fortune

- When fortune comes to you, offer her a chair.

- If it rains fortune, you must hold your dish.

Freedom

- To be poor *"poe"* and free is better than to be wealthy *"gentri"* and confined.

Friend, Comrade, Acquaintance

- A friend is one who knows everything about you and still wants to be a friend.

- A friend in need is a friend indeed.

- If you have true friends, you are wealthy.

- Try your friends before you trust them.

- Do not trust a new friend or an old enemy.

Good, Good Quality, Excellent, Superior

- A good example is the best sermon.

- A good example is the best example.

- A good beginning is half the battle.

- A good building has a good foundation.

Good Cooking, Food Preparation, Cookery, Cuisine

- Good cooking is a woman's path to a man's heart.

- The way to a man's heart is through his stomach.

Gossip, News, Information, Rumor, Hearsay, Chattering

- It is true that she was assigned a gossip bench "*kongosar bench.*"

- What is said over a dead lion's body cannot be said when he is alive.

- If you want to gossip in the community; wear a Creole traditional female African dress called "*kabarslot*" and carry a Creole drawstring, cloth purse called "*kotoku.*"

- When you want to abuse a deaf man, do not abuse him in the presence of his child.

- He who doesn't like chattering "*talk talk*" women must stay a bachelor.

- A lie has no legs, but it has wings.

- He who spreads rumors with you will also talk about you.

- The mouth of a woman takes no holiday.

- Flash your news on a bamboo winnowing fan "*fanner*"; it will be blown away and even spread like wild fire.

- The ruin of a nation begins in the homes of its people.

- Word does not have ears "*yais*," but it hears from afar.

- If you listen to the noise of the market, you won't buy your fish.

- News has no feet, but it travels.

- No news is good news.

- Unless you call out, who will open the door?

- When you want to hear the necessary information from the community, stay around your enemy.

- It takes more than one person to gossip.

- His attitude and behavior are like a dilapidated house "*broke os.*"

- If you want to spread the news like wildfire in the community, wear a Creole traditional female African dress called "*kabarslot*" and carry a Creole drawstring cloth purse, called "*kotuku.*"

Grateful, Appreciative, Thankful

- A dog never forgets its master.

- A dog returns to where it has been fed.

- If you fall for me, I will fall for you

- One good turn deserves another.

- We know the worth of water after the well is dry.

- You do not bite the finger that feeds you.

- If you stretch out your hand, another hand will be stretched out to you in return.

- No matter how far a stream flows, it never forgets its source.

- Any river that forgets its source will definitely dry up.

- Do not fill up the well that supplies your water.

- Do not kill the goose that lays the golden egg.

- Do not forget the bridge that you cross over.

- Do not burn the bridge that you cross over.

- Never abuse the bridge that you cross.

- A good dog deserves a good bone.

- Thanks cost nothing.

Greed, Avarice, Covetousness, Selfishness, Egotism

- He who hunts two rats "*aratar*" catches none.

- He who hunts two birds "*bord*" catches none.

- He comes in like a wind, and goes out like a wind.

- He who wants everything will lose everything.

- Invite someone into your parlor; he/she will try to occupy your bedroom.

- He who throws a stone "*tone*" to catch two birds "*bord*" catches none.

- How much can one man consume on ten-penny salt?

- A dog has four feet, but he cannot travel on four roads at once.

- No matter how full the river, it still wants to swell more.

Grief, Sorrow, Heartache, Pain

- Time softens grief.

Group, Company, Union, Band

- Monkey speaks; monkey understands.

- Monkeys are by party; pigeons are by pair.

- If you lie with a dog, you will get up with fleas.

- A dog gives birth to a dog.

- However tightly packed a house might be, a hen "*fol*" will always find somewhere to lay her eggs "*aigê.*"

- Evil knows where evil sleeps.

- Birds "*bord*" of the same feather flock together.

- As long as you stay in a group, the lion will stay hungry.

- When there is no enemy within, the enemies outside will not hurt you.

Guilt, Responsibility, Fault

- He who is guilty is the one that has much to say.

- Try this bracelet; if it fits you wear it, but if it hurts you, throw it away no matter how shiny.

- Try this coat; if it fits you, wear it!

Habit, Practice, Custom, Pattern, Routine

- A monkey will never leave its black hands.

- A chameleon "*komehel*" can only change its color but never changes its skin.

- A cat "*puss*" may go to a monastery, but it is still a cat "*puss*."

- A leopard "*lepet*" will never change its spots.

- Never wrestle with a pig "*hog*" in the mud "*portor-portor*"; both of you will get dirty, and the pig "*hog*" will like it.

- This is what a dirty boy "*dote boy*" expects to see or to hear; the tap is closed!

- If you are wrestling with a pig "*hog*" in the mud "*portor-portor*," you will never win.

- A wood will remain forever in the river but will never be a crocodile.

- An orange "*orinch*" never produces lime "*lem*."

- You do not teach an old dog a new trick.

- You do not teach the path of the forest to an old gorilla.

- A bad habit is like fire; you can't play with it and expect not to get burned.

- A dog does not mind being called a dog.

- Rain beats a leopard's "*lepet*" skin, but it does not wash out its spots.

- You can take a man out of a jungle, but you cannot take the jungle out of a man.

- A thief will always be a thief.

- Habit becomes nature.

- The pumpkin vine never bears watermelons.

- Water does not skip a hole.

Happiness, Contentment, Pleasure, Joy

- Happiness is the place between too little and too much.

- Be happy; don't worry.

- The key to happiness and success is to have a dream.

Hardships, The Storms of Life

- When you fall, dust yourself off and try again.

- When you fall, try to be on your feet, or else someone will trample on you.

- Do not look where you fell but where you slipped.

- Blood is running down the dog's eyes.

Hatred, Extreme Dislike

- There is no medicine to cure hatred.

- A thief doesn't like a thief.

Heart, Mind, Tenderness, Kindness, Feeling, Sympathy, Empathy, Affection

- Loving hearts have gentle hands.

- Heavy hearts; heavy steps.

- Bad mind, bad heart.

Hint, Insinuate, Imply, Allude To, Refer To

- Hint knows its master and "*Kabarslot*," a long Creole traditional, female African dress, knows its mistress "*misses*."

Hope, Trust, Anticipate

- Hope is the pillar of the world.

Hospitality, Warmth, Generosity, Welcome, Kindness

- However tightly packed a house might be, a hen "*fol*" will always find somewhere to lay its eggs "aigê".

Humble, Modest, Meek

- A good name is better than gold.

- He who positions himself under your feet is modest.

- A man who is on his knees is taller than the trees.

- He stands the longest that kneels lowest.

- A child "*pickin*" who knows how to wash his hands will eat with a king.

Hungry, Starving

- I would rather have an upset stomach than waste a delicious food.

- Hunger is felt by a slave and hunger is felt by a king.

- The tummy "*belle*" does not have a mirror.

- He who does not cultivate his field will die of hunger.

- A hungry man is an angry man.

Ignorant, Unaware, Badly Informed, Bad-Mannered, Rude

- He who is carried does not realize how far the town is.

- It is an insult to be ignorant.

- If you fail to carry an item, you will not realize that it is very heavy.

- What you don't know, you will not recognize.

- What you don't know will not hurt you.

- Ignorant is a cuss.

- If you boast of your own knowledge, you show your ignorance.

- Half an education is more dangerous than no education.

- Not to know is bad, but don't want to know is even worse.

- The corpse does not know the cost of her shroud.

Ignore, Disregard, Snub
- It is when you look at a bride's face *"yahwo face,"* you will know that she is crying.

Immorality, Dishonesty
- The ax forgets; the tree remembers.

- What forgets is the ax, but the tree that has been axed will never forget.

- He who cleans excreta *"pu-pu"* remembers.

Imperfect, Defective, Deficient, Faulty
- Even the most beautiful woman is not perfect.

- The horse has four feet, but it falls anyway.

Impossible, Impractical
- You will not take nut oil *"nat-ty"* to fry stone.

- If you cannot find a black sheep during the day, you will never find it at night.

- No one looks for a needle in a haystack.

- No one places a square peg in a round hole.

- Dating a married man, you are trying to carry water in a basket.

Inferior, Mediocre, Second-Rate, Lower, Lesser

- No one can make you feel inferior without your consent.

- Your attitude or behavior reveals whether you will be selected to prepare a pot of African cassava paste, "*fufu/foo-foo*" during an African feast or ceremony known as; "*Awujoh or Awujor*".

Indulge, Spoil, Pamper

- Give a calf enough rope, and it will hang itself.

Influence, Pressure, Sway, Control, Manipulate, Convince, Affect, Win Over

- Birds "*bord*" of the same feather flock together.

- One rotten bean is enough to spoil the entire sauce.

- One rotten apple spoils the rest.

- When you fall into the river, you must swim.

- If you lie down with a dog, you will get up with fleas.

- When the iron is hot, you can either mold it into different shapes or cut it into separate pieces.

- When visiting a country where the people dance on one foot, you should dance on one foot.

- If you go with wolves, you will learn to howl.

- It is an iron that cuts another iron.

- Do not fall into the river and turn into a fish.

- Misery likes company.

Injustice, Slavery

- A monkey works, and a baboon *"babu"* receives the reward.

- The deprived worked very hard, but the wealthy named *"Yando"* received the reward.

- An infectious tropical disease, *"craw-craw,"* is no slave for an infectious tropical disease, *"yaws."*

- One cannot look after a dog if the government owns it.

- One cannot ride a willing horse to death.

- The turtle or tortoise *"trukie"* says that the world is not a level ground.

- The jackass says that the world is not a level ground.

- In the fowl's *"fol"* court, a cockroach *"kackroach"* never wins its case.

- In the court of law, the jackass never wins its case.

- Do not think that I am a jackass!

- What is good luck for someone is bad luck for another.

- Even the fingers are not equal.

- The head of a sheep is different from a goat's head.

Insensitive, Hard, Thick-Skinned

- Man is like palm wine: when young, sweet but without strength; in old age, strong but harsh.

Insinuate, Imply, Implicate

-   Hint knows its master, and a dress "*kabarslot,*" *a Creole African female dress*, knows its misses.

Insufficient, Deficient, Not Enough

-   A khaki material is not enough to sew the station master's uniform and the porter is requesting a long-pants uniform.

-   A food for one man is starvation for two.

Inspiration, Motivation, Encouragement, Stimulation

-   When God is for you, the devil "*deble*" can't do you any harm.

-   If God is for you, who will be against you? No one!

-   Behind a great man there is a great woman.

Interfere, Obstruct, Get in the Way

-   A person is a guest for one or two days, but becomes an intruder on the third day.

-   If it is not broken, do not try to fix it.

-   Trying to count white-color yams by the dozen, and here rolls some coco yams!

Investment, Asset, Savings

-   Children "*pickin*" are the reward of life.

Involve, Engage, Engross

-   One does not cross a river without getting wet.

- Dance according to the music.

- Move your neck according to the beat of the drum.

- He who slits a piece of cloth will know how to sew it together again.

- If you are not part of the solution, you are part of the problem.

Justice, Fairness, Honesty, Integrity

- What is good for the goose is good for the gander.

Kindness, Gentleness

- We have seen today; tomorrow is in the hands of God.

- A good name can buy things that money cannot buy.

- A good word produces the best kola nut.

- When a road is good, it is used the second time.

- Kindness heals wounds.

- A river sometimes overflows; so does kindness.

Knowledge, Facts, Comprehension, Information, Understanding, Realization, Wisdom, Experience, Awareness, Familiarity, Know-How, Skill

- He who does not know one thing knows another.

- Knowledge is like a garden: if it is not cultivated, it cannot be harvested.

- The shoe knows if the stocking has a hole.

- The foot knows where the shoe pinches.

- Knowledge without practice makes but half an artist.

- If you do not know someone, then you will call him, you!

- When a man is coming toward you, you need not say, come here!

- The gum understands the teeth's "*teet*" affairs.

- Even before a bird flies, one can identify the amount of eggs in its stomach.

- Knowledge is power.

- Knowledge is better than riches.

- Strive for knowledge but fewer words. *"Karpu sense nor karpu word."*

Laziness, Apathy, Idleness, Lethargy, Lack of Interest

- He who does not cultivate his field will die of hunger.

- Money "*korpor*" does not grow on trees "*tick*"; one earns his living by working.

- Grass does not grow on the nose of a thief.

- Those who play with chicks will by no means fly with eagles.

- A chattering "*talk talk*" bird builds no nest.

- A sleepy fox catches no chicken.

Learn, Gain Knowledge, Be Taught, Be Trained, Discover, Understand

- He who learns, teaches.

Lie, Dishonesty, Deceit, Fabrication, Deception

- When your mouth stumbles, it is worse than feet.

- To speak rudely is better than lying smoothly.

- A lie has no legs, but it has wings.

- We don't believe a liar when he speaks the truth.

- A liar needs a good memory.

- A liar does not believe anyone.

Life, Existence

- Without life there is nothing.

- Life is but an empty dream.

- Life can seem ungrateful and not always kind.

- Life can place challenges right at your feet.

- Life is short and full of blisters.

- Life can surround you with people who care.

- Life clearly does offer its ups and its downs.

- Life's days can bring you both smiles and frowns.

- Life teaches us to take the good with the bad.

- Life is a shadow and a mist; it passes quickly by, and is no more.

- Life is a mixture of happy and sad.

- Life is a storm.

- Life is precious.

Like, Be Fond Of, Enjoy

- Don't do what you like, but like what you do.

Listen, Pay Attention

- A good listener hears a good speaker.

Loss, Unluckiness

- A drowning man will clutch at a straw.

Love, Adore, Be Devoted To, Worship

- To love someone who does not love you is like shaking water on a duck's back.

- Love is like a fatty substance in a soup. It is only sweet when it is hot.

- Do not be so much in love that you cannot tell when it starts raining.

- When one is in love, a cliff becomes a meadow.

- Love is like an egg; if you want to really enjoy it, you should not hold it too hard or too lightly.

- Love is like a baby; it needs to be treated tenderly.

- Love is like rice, transplanted but still grows.

- Let your love be like a misty rain drizzling but flooding into the river.

- It is better to be loved than to be feared.

- It is better to have loved than not to have loved at all.

- To love someone who does not love you, is like shaking a tree to make the dewdrops fall.

- Love a man; love his dog.

- Love a dog; love his tail.

- Love does not realize a bent hip.

- Love at first sight saves a lot of time.

Luck, Fortune, Destiny

- What is good luck for someone might be bad luck for another.

Lovers, Devotion

- It is easier to revitalize two lovers' relations.

- Old firewood ignites faster.

Man, Gentleman, Guy, Chap, Male

- The tongue of an idle man is never idle.

- Do not trust a hasty man.

- A bad husband is not a good man.

- A small boy is a pain in the neck; an older man is a pain in the heart.

- A discouraged man is a defeated man.

- A man on his knees is taller than the trees.

- Man is like palm wine: when young, sweet but without strength; in old age, strong but harsh.

- Behind a great man there is a great woman.

- Pride is a magnifying glass men use.

- A man without a wife is like a vase without flowers.

Marriage, Matrimony, Wedding

- Marriage is better than waking up next to an empty pillow.

- A bad marriage is better than a good divorce.

- Marriage is not a fast knot but a slip knot.

- Marriage is to keep secrets, secret.

- Marriage is keeping secrets, secret, so that each one's back will be covered.

- Marriage is commitment.

- Marriage is working hand in hand.

- Marriage is love.

Miser, Saver

- Death is the key that will open the miser's coffin.

Mistake, Fault, Error

- Do not look where you fell, but where you slipped.

- Mistakes are good teachers.

Money, Currency, Cash

- If the palm of the hand itches, it signifies the coming of great luck.

- He who loves money must labor.

- Money has wings.

- Money is sharper than a sword.

- A good thing sells itself, but a bad thing advertises itself.

Motivation, Inspiration, Drive

- The bird "*bord*" that arrives early catches the most worms.

- The horse that arrives early by the river drinks the best water.

Need, Require, Want, Necessitate

- He who is sick will not refuse to see the doctor.

Nosy, Taking Notice of Anything

- Ears "*yais*" have no cover-up.

- Why arguing over the cost of a pig "*hog*" and your dad "*dadie or papa*" is not a butcher?

- The eyes that see everything else see not themselves.

Nuture, Care For, Look After, Take Care Of, Raise, Love, Rear, Foster

- It takes a village to raise up a child.

- Opportunity once lost will never be regained.

Over, Complete, Finished, Terminated, Greater Than, Larger Than, More, In Excess Of, More Than

- It is the final straw that breaks the camel's back.

- A bowl of palava/palaver sauce "*plassas*" surpasses a plate of cooked rice.

- A cup of water surpasses a bowl of flour.

Ownership, Possession, Rights

- A broken canoe "*brok-o-cunu*" in a wharf has its owner.

Past, History, Earlier Period

- The past is certain but not forgotten.

Patient, Tolerant

- An awful husband sleeping beside his wife is better than an empty bed.

- Move a little bit *"Boe push lili bit"* is better than a wife sleeping on an empty bed.

- There is no bad bush to get rid of an awful child *"pickin."*

- Bring a pot of yams to a boil, and patiently search for a knife *"nef."*

- A bird *"bord"* in the hand is worth two in the bush.

- Even the teeth and the tongue *"teet en tongue"* sometimes come into conflict, but they will always unite to chew.

- A very long road will certainly come to an end.

- Even a broken canoe *"brok-o-cunu"* in a wharf is better than an empty wharf.

- A bedmate who sleeps on the other side of the bed is better than being alone in bed.

- A husband with a wife is better than a bachelor.

- A wife with a husband is better than a spinster.

- A friend who frowns is better than an enemy who smiles.

- A very long excreta *"pu-pu"* will dissociate at a point.

- A family *"fambul"* tree sometimes bends, but it never breaks.

- The devil *"deble"* that you know is better than the angel you have not seen.

- A patient dog eats the best bone.

- No matter how long the night, the day is sure to come.

- No matter how long the winter is, spring is sure to follow.

- If you look down slowly, you see the bridge of your nose.

- Hope is the pillar of the world.

- God does not sleep.

- Little drops of rain each day will fill the river to overflowing.

- An old broom sweeps clean.

- It takes a whole village to bring up a child.

- It is the wife who knows her husband.

- Marriage is not a fast knot but a slipped knot.

- Not all the flowers of a tree produce fruit.

- Only the pew can tell when the sermon is interesting. If the sermon is not interesting, one feels the hardness of the pew while sitting.

- Spilled water is better than a broken jar.

- A one-eyed man is better than none.

- Place a mortar and pestle *"martar odoe en martar pensul"* behind your back door to secure your house and wait for a thief.

- He is giving him a long rope.

- Take embarrassment and eat *"bet"* a caterpillar *"fatfut."*

- If you are patient when dissecting an ant *"anch,"* you will see its intestines *"guts."*

- It is little by little that a bird *"bord"* builds its nest.

- There is no bad bush to throw away a bad child *"pickin."*

- Rome was not built in a day.

- The best way to eat an elephant in your path is to cut it up into little pieces.

- However long the night, the dawn will break.

- Though the road is very long, it will curve to a certain point.

- Tie a cow with a long rope.

- An untrustworthy husband or wife is better than waking up next to an empty pillow "*pilar.*"

- When the door of happiness closes, another one opens.

Payment, Gain, Benefit, Profit

- Fine words do produce good kola nut.

Peace, Calm, Tranquility

- Peace is costly, but it is worth the expense.

- Where there is no wood, the fire goes out.

- Open heart and open mind.

Perfect, Just Right, Wonderful, Great

- He who waits for perfect conditions will never get anything done.

Perpetual, Permanent

- A paddle here, a paddle there, the canoe stays still.

- Travel here and travel there, but the riverside stone "*watar sy tone*" is still in its position.

- The stone that the builders rejected has become the very corner stone.

Persistence, Determination, Perseverance

- The leaf that tastes sweet in a goat's mouth is the leaf that will give the goat an upset stomach.

- A strong disease needs a strong medicine.

- By trying, the monkey learns to jump from tree to tree.

Personality, Self-Esteem, Self-Image, Opinion of Yourself

- An ego trip will never get you anywhere.

Pest, A Pain in the Neck

- A woman is like a blanket: if you cover yourself with it, it bothers you; if you throw it aside, you will feel the cold.

- Give me a push from my back does not mean to give me a hunchback.

Pleasant, Good, Kind, Polite, Fine

- When a road is good, it is used the second time.

Prejudice, Discrimination, Bigotry

- You must not judge the book by its cover.

- You must judge a man by the work of his hands.

- You do not like a dog and hate its tail.

- The jackass says the world is not level.

- Don't hang a man by his looks.

Pride

- To be poor and free is better than to be a rich slave.

- A peacock is always displaying its beautiful feathers.

- He who is called a man must behave like a man.

- If you do not want the monkey's tail to touch you, do not join the monkey's dance.

- How much can one man consume on ten-penny salt?

- You are seeing the skin of the potato because you are really full.

- He who refuses a gift will not fill his barn.

- Pride only goes the length one can spit.

- Pride goes before destruction.

- Pride goes; shame follows.

- Pride is the magnifying glass men use.

- If you see what the duck eats, then you eat no more duck.

- The horse is not too good to carry its hay.

- The elephant never gets tired of carrying its tusks.

Priority, Main Concern

- When your house is burning, there is no time to go hunting.

- A man whose house is on fire does not go hunting for a rat.

- If you watch your pot, your food will not burn.

Problem, Crisis, Dilemma, Trouble, Setback

- Problem or setback is like a bone stuck in your throat.

Problem To Be Solved

- If you are not part of the solution, you are part of the problem.

- We have a bone to pick.

- We have a fish to fry.

- She has a big fish for you to fry.

- A loose tooth will not rest until it is pulled.

- God will not give you an assignment that you will not be able to accomplish.

Proverbs, Idioms, Sayings

- Proverbs are the palm oil with which words are eaten.

- Proverbs, parables, and wise sayings are the daughters of experience.

- A man who knows proverbs will reconcile differences.

- A proverb is the horse that can carry one swiftly to the discovery of ideas.

- A proverb is the horse of conversation; when the conversation lags, a proverb revives it.

- Proverbs, parables, and wise sayings are the experiences of life.

Publicize, Broadcast, Make Known, Announce

- The ruin of a nation begins in the homes of its people.

- Home affairs are not talked about in the public square.

- Publish your joys instead of your troubles.

- Unless the home affairs are talked about, the public will not be aware of the situation.

- In a matter of fact, he does not place his mouth on a bottle's spout when speaking; he speaks openly.

- In fact, he does not place his mouth in a hole; he publicizes.

- If you do not have a product to sell, what will they buy?

- Unless you open the window; who will see you?

- Unless you call out, who will open the door?

Purposeless, Meaningless, Empty

- A home without a woman is like a barn without cattle.

Quarrel, Argue, Squabble, Clash

- When you see a toad "*uporlor*" climbing a tree, you must know the ground is hot.

- It takes two to tangle.

- If nothing touches the palm leaves, they do not rustle.

- It takes two to make a quarrel "*kartar-kartar or plabar.*"

- One finger cannot grab hold of a louse "*loss*" on someone's head.

- A single bracelet does not jingle.

- She is known as Sarah palaver "*plabar.*"

- A quarrel ends, but words spoken never die.

- A goat excretion "*pu-pu*" feels like rolling down a hill but waits for someone to give it a push.

- Even the tongue and the teeth "*tongue en teet*" quarrel sometimes!

- You are fighting a losing battle.

- It takes two hands to wash a back.

- To engage in conflict, one does not bring a knife that cuts but a needle that sews.

- When you see clouds gathering, prepare to catch rainwater.

- One monkey does not start a show.

- Wood already touched by fire is not hard to set aflame.

- It takes an act to have dirty water.

- If you tell two people to live together, you are telling them to quarrel.

- A bird "*bord*" wants to fly but waits for the leaves to shake.

- The fire is really hot!

Quiet, Silence, Calm

- Place your feet in your mouth.

- Bite your tongue "*bet u tongue.*"

- A mouth which eats does not talk.

- If you are in hiding, do not light a fire.

- One must talk little, and listen more.

- Silence is golden.

- If you grow up among wise men, you will find out that there is nothing better for man than silence.

- Leave a bowl of palaver/palava sauce "*plassas*" for a plate of cooked rice.

- He who closes the door will open it when it is time.

- If you don't have something good to say, don't say anything.

- Let me hear as far as I can.

Reckless, Careless, Inattentive, Irresponsible

-   He who does not mend his clothes will soon have none.

Reconcile, Settle, Resolve, Patch Up, Bring Together

-   Let us bury the hatchet.

-   Let sleeping dogs lie.

-   When vines intertwine your roof, it is time to cut them down.

-   Any nature of crying is good for a funeral.

-   He who upsets someone should know how to patch things up.

-   Teeth and tongue *"teet en tongue"* do collide but later solve their problems.

-   Let us throw away the coals of fire.

-   Instead of burning the item, wet it through.

Regenerate, Renew, Reawaken, Relight, Rekindle, Revive

-   Old friendship is not hard to rekindle.

-   Old firewood is easy to relight.

Remember, Keep in Mind

-   An elephant does not forget.

Respect, Admiration, High Opinion, Reverence

-   To command respect is better than a full stomach.

-   A poor man's *"poe man"* hat does not last long, because he takes it off too often to pay his respects.

- You do not teach the path of the forest to an old gorilla.

- It is how you dress up your mask-devil that it will be respected.

- The okra "*okro*" plant will never get taller than its master, the sower.

- Two masters will not steer one ship.

- No matter how angry a policeman, he will never smack his boss.

- What is said over the dead lion's body could not be said when it was alive.

- Cross the road before you talk about the crocodile's mother.

- A child "*pickin*" who knows how to wash his hands will eat with a king.

- If you don't want a monkey's tail to touch you, don't participate in the monkey's dance.

- Virtue is better than wealth.

- It is the duty of the children to wait on the oldest member of the family "*fambul*," and not the oldest on children.

- Familiarity breeds contempt, but distance breeds respect.

- A child will never be older than his/her father.

- A dog knows its master.

- The African cassava paste, "*fufu/foo-foo*," does not disrespect okra soup "*okro soup*."

- Never let a boy "*bor-bor*" do a man's work.

- Never mistake a chicken shit for an egg.

- Do nothing to make you lose respect for yourself.

- Respect is a two-way street.

- Respect is earned.

- Don't price yourself too cheap.

- Even a fallen cotton tree is taller than a weed or grass.

- No matter how old you are, you can never be older than your father.

- One camel does not make fun of the other camel's hump.

- Know thyself is better than good advice.

- You will be assessed or evaluated by the way you portray yourself.

- If you don't lie down on the floor, no one can walk on you.

- No one can make you feel inferior without your consent.

- Even a frog "*uporlor*" with a full stomach will never disrespect a vulture "*yubar.*"

- An older person "*ol-man*" will be enthusiastic to sit and discuss with a respectful child "*pickin.*"

Reveal, Disclose, Make Known

- If you burn a house, can you conceal the smoke?

- If you are hiding, don't light a fire.

Rich, Wealthy, Well-Off, Prosperous

- To be rich is determination and hard work.

Rock, The Tower of Strength

- The hip is sometimes insignificant until it is infected.

Rogue, Parasite, Rascal, Good-for-Nothing, Crook, Scoundrel

- A rat knows where another rat lives.

Secret, Undisclosed, Hush-Hush

- Wash or keep your dirty linen at home.

- A dog's dream will never be revealed.

- Keep secrets, secret.

- Secrets and lies are the blades that can cut and divide a relationship.

Seeing Is Believing, Perceive, Catch Sight Of, Set Eyes On

- You do not buy a pig "*hog*" in a pen.

- You do not buy a boat that is under water.

- You do not buy a cow only by the sound of its voice.

- Choose your neighbors before you buy your house.

- Don't buy salt without licking it.

- You do not leap in the dark.

Self-Conscious, Awkward, Embarrassed, Insecure, Unsure of Yourself

- When a man has a large nose, he thinks others are talking about it.

Self-Doubting, Insecure, Uncertain

- Still water runs deep.

- It is when a leopard "*lepet*" is wet that any animal will play around.

Self-Esteem, Self-Worth, Sense of Worth, Confidence, Self-Respect
- What costs little is little esteemed.

Sense, Intelligence, Brains, Intellect, Logic
- Good judgment is better than words. *"Karpu sense nor karpu word."*

Sensitive, Aware, Responsive, Receptive
- If a man born with a cut-off nose is around the neighborhood, why should someone cease to say, "Hmmmm"?
- When a man has a large nose, he thinks others are talking about it.

Separate, Disconnect
- If you are the cup handle, beware of the cup.

Serious, Not Funny
- Teeth *"teet"* do not mourn.

Silly, Foolish, Stupid
- You may hide the fire, but what about the smoke?
- The beggar that begs near another beggar will never be rich.
- It is a slave who will work as a Lagos laborer.
- A fool and his money is one big party.
- A fool and his money will soon be parted.
- If you make yourself into a doormat, people will wipe their feet on you.

- A silly daughter teaches her mother how to bear children.

- A dimwit will surely wash his face from his chin to his forehead.

- It takes the first child in the family to be silly.

Similar, Alike, Akin, Of the Same Kind

- Excreta cannot restrict other excreta to reside in an open grass field.

- Evil knows where evil sleeps.

Single, Alone, Solitary, Lonely, Friendless

- *I am a lamppost "palampo."*

Smart, Neat, Tidy, Stylish, Well-Dressed, Clever, Intelligent

- A sensible person laughs while abused, but a fool would be annoyed.

- A bird "*bord*" doesn't alert his fellow bird "*bord*" that a stone is coming.

- A barber does not shave himself.

- A monkey knows which branch to swim from.

- If you climb up a tree, you must climb down the tree.

- Water always finds a way out.

- He who lives in the attic knows where the roof leaks.

- When you want to hear the necessary information from the community, stay around your enemy.

Smile, Grin

- Smile and give the whole world sunshine.

- Smile and the world will smile with you.

- You are not fully dressed until you wear a smile.

- Make the miles short with smiles.

- The vulgar man grins, but does not smile.

Solve, Resolve, Get to the Bottom of the Problem, Answer

- The bowl and the calabash are yours; mix the contents into a desired consistency.

Source, Informer, Spokesperson

- It is from the horse's mouth.

Sorrow, Grief, Sadness, Distress

- Sorrow is like a precious treasure shown only to relatives and friends.

Spotlight, Stand Out, Center of Attention

- Every dog has his day.

Stop, Finish, Terminate

- A very long road will certainly come to an end.

- Though the road is very long, it will curve to a certain point.

Strive, Endeavor, Go All-Out, Try Hard, Do Your Best, Make Every Effort

- Whatever you are, be a good one.

- Be the best that you can be.

- You do not have to be the sharpest knife in the bunch, but do your best.

- He excels above everyone's expectations.

- Strive to accomplish your dreams.

Strong, Muscular, Tough

- A big fish is caught with big bait.

- A strong individual does not go around fighting.

Stubborn, Headstrong

- A chicken "*fol*" that is not afraid of the sound "*SH-E-E-E*," to leave a specific area will be afraid of stones thrown at it.

- Even the night has ears "*yais.*"

- Even flies have ears "*yais.*"

- Old sores are hard to cure.

- Mothers are hard of hearing.

- Do not throw water over a duck's back.

- A child "*pickin*" who refuses to listen to her mother "*mama*" will be brought up roughly in the street.

- You can lead a horse to the river, but you cannot make the horse drink the water.

- The food that is sweet in a goat's mouth will give him a loose bowel movement.

- You cannot take a horse to a river to drink water when it is not thirsty.

- A child *"pickin"* who tries to let his mother have sleepless nights, will not sleep either.

- You will not continue to beat the baboon *"babu"* because of it ugliness.

- A child *"pickin"* who tries to wear his father's pants *"trousers or trosis"* will continue to adjust the waistline with a string.

Success, Victory, Achievement, Triumph, Accomplishment

- Each of us has two ends, a sitting end and a thinking end; success depends on which one we use.

- Determination, hard work, and discipline are the keys to success.

- Success is an ongoing process but not an end.

- Success is a journey, not a destination.

Support, Backing, Assistance, Encouragement

- It takes a village or the support of a whole African village to bring up a child *"pickin."*

Survive, Endure, Stay Alive, Someone Wins and Someone Loses, Ups and Downs

- Every bird flies with its own wings.

- A child will not die because his/her mother's breast milk has dried up.

- A mind is like a bag; everyone carries his/her own.

- When you have no one to watch you, watch yourself.

- Let everyone paddle his own canoe.

- In the dog's world, dog will eat dog.

- It is the dog eat dog's world.

- In a dog's world, survival is for the fittest.

- In the fish world, fish will eat fish.

- In the monkey's world, each monkey jumps for itself.

- Every man is for himself, and God for all.

- The mind is like a bag, everyone carries his/her own.

Suspect, Infer, Distrust, Mistrust, Be Suspicious Of

- Try this bracelet; if it fits you wear it, but if it hurts you, throw it away no matter how shiny.

- A thief *"akatar"* is always under suspicion.

- Where there is smoke, there is fire.

Switch, Swop, Swap, Substitute, Alter

- The music changes; so does the dance.

Talk, Chat, Converse, Gossip, Speak, Discuss

- In fact, he does not place his mouth on the spout of a bottle; he voices out his opinion.

- In a matter of fact, he does not place his mouth in a hole; he speaks his mind.

- Empty barrels make the most noise.

- Talk less and say more.

Teacher, Educator, Instructor, Professor, Lecturer, Coach, Tutor

- Many teachers, few scholars.

- Experience is a great teacher.

- Mistakes make a great teacher.

Temporary, Impermanent, Transitory

- Every leaf will wither away eventually.

- Even in time, every ordinary leaf rots.

Thief, Burglar, Shoplifter, Robber, Pickpocket

- Set a thief *"akartar"* to catch a thief *"akartar."*

- Thief, thief; God laughs.

- A blade won't cut another blade; a cheat won't cheat another cheat.

- Leave a cat *"puss"* to watch a plate of fish.

- Rats know the way of other rats.

- The witness of a rat is another rat.

- Leave a cat *"puss"* to watch a bowl of milk.

Thrifty, Cheap, Economical

- He is as cheap as the backside of a spoon.

Time, Instance, Occasion, Period, Moment

- Time and tide wait for no man.

- Time may be your friend or your enemy.

- If the tide goes out, it will come in again.

- Time is a healer.

Today, Now, At the Moment, At Present

- Build your house; then think of your furniture.

- An egg today is better than a hen tomorrow.

- You are what you are, not what you were.

- No time like now.

- Don't prepare for a rainy day without enjoying today's sunshine.

- We are here today and gone tomorrow.

Togetherness, Unity

- A family "*fambul*" is like a thick forest; often from outside it is dense, and when you are inside, each tree has its own position.

- Where there is no enemy within, the enemy outside cannot hurt you.

- It takes a whole village to bring up a child.

- A man cannot offer to sweep the street leaving his house a mess.

- Don't hesitate to tell a lie that will unite husband and wife who have been separated. But don't tell the truth that will bring enmity in the family.

- When spiderwebs unite, they can tie up a lion

- Birds "*bord*" of the same feather flock together.

- Cross the river in a crowd, and the crocodile won't eat you.

- However tightly packed a house might be, a hen "*fol*" finds a corner to lay her eggs "*aigê*."

Tomorrow

- No one has seen tomorrow.

- Tomorrow never comes.

Tough, Dangerous, Risky

- You cannot scare a monkey with a dead baboon "*dy babu.*"

- The lion does not turn around when a small dog barks.

Treacherous, Untrustworthy, Deceitful, Unfaithful, Disloyal

- Still water runs deep.

- It is the calm and silent water that drowns the man.

- Confiding a secret to an unworthy person is like carrying a bag with a hole.

- She is like a road, pretty and crooked.

- He/she is a green snake in green grass.

- Where there is smoke, there is fire.

- He/she is like a termite " *bug-bug*" that eats the inside of a wood and leaves the outside untouched.

Tricky, Crafty, Devious, Sly, Deceitful, Cunning

- A monkey does not forget the color of his hands.

- Water always finds a way out.

- When a cunning man dies, it is a cunning man who buries him.

- A trick is smoke; you cannot conceal it.

Trouble, Difficulty, Trial, Tribulation, Dilemma, Problem

- Don't tie a toad "*uporlor*" around your foot while running from a snake.

- Trouble is a bitter tree, but sometimes it produces good fruits.

- Unexpected rainfall allows goats and sheep to seek shelter under the same roof.

- An animal with a long tail should not dance near a trap.

- Rain does not fall on one roof alone.

- Eggs "*aigê*" have no business dancing with stones.

- Dance to the beat of the drum.

- A pig "*hog*" asked his mother, "mom, '*mama*' why is my mouth so long?" "Wait, you will find out". His mother replied.

- When you provoke a snake, then you realize it can stand straight up.

- A hawk's "*ack*" happiness is not a chicken's "*fol*" happiness.

- All lizards "*kondo*" crawl with bellies on the ground, but it is very difficult to detect the lizard with an upset belly.

- He who marries a beauty marries trouble.

- One who digs too deep for a fish will come out with a snake.

- To stumble is not to fall.

- When you fall, dust yourself off and try again.

- When you fall, try to be on your feet, or else someone will trample on you.

- When one is in trouble, one remembers God.

- Restless feet may walk into a snake pit.

- It is the trouble of the world that allows the monkey to chew hot, spicy peppers.

- Cast your cares on the Almighty; he will be up all night anyway.

- Cast your troubles *"**wahalar**"* on the Lord, and he will be up all night anyway.

- Do not allow me to skip with one foot.

- Do not place a knife *"nef"* on my throat.

- We are paddling the same canoe.

- Even an iron spoon has a curved shape!

- A heap of sand spilled in your bowl of farina *"gari"*!

- In the fowl's *"fol"* country, each fowl *"fol"* snatches what it can and runs away with it.

- Trouble *"wahalar"* is felt by the wealthy; trouble *"**w**ahalar"* is also felt by the poor.

- Trouble can make you or break you.

- Don't fish in troubled water.

- Trouble *"wahalar"* literally filled a basket known as Oku basket *"Oku bly."*

- If there is a spark, there is a fire. there will be a fire.

- The fire is really hot!

Trust, Hope, Faith, Confidence, Reliance

- An enjoyable wedding party is determined by the bachelor's eve celebration.

- Don't always tell the truth, but never tell a lie.

Trustworthy, Honest, Reliable, Truthful, Faithful, Responsible

- In order to keep your neighbor honest, lock your door.

Truth, Fact, Reality

- The truth is sometimes difficult to say.

- Truth may be blamed, but not shamed.

- The truth always hurts.

- You will know the truth, and the truth will set you free.

- Truth and honesty are the foundation of relationship.

Unafraid

- When the mouse "*aratar*" laughs at the cat "*puss,*" there's a hole nearby.

Understand, Know, Get the Picture, Be Familiar With

- It is a Creole spoon that is utilized to stir a Creole soup.

- To understand someone is to live with someone.

- You are the only one that is beating and dancing to the drum.

- What's inside a coco-yam or yam that the knife does not know?

- What's in a pumpkin that the knife does not know?

- The gums understand the teeth "*teet*" affairs.

- When a man is walking toward you, you need not say, come here!

- Only a monkey understands a monkey.

- Monkey talks; monkey listens.

Unequal, Uneven, Disproportionate, Imbalanced, Unfair

- All fingers are not the same size.

Unfortunate, Unlucky, Inopportune

- I am Charlotte "*Shalat*"! I am always the unfortunate one.

Ungrateful

- Do not tell a man who is carrying you that he stinks.

- He who is carried does not realize the distance.

- He who is carried on another's back does not appreciate how far off the town is.

- Do not call the forest that shelters you a jungle.

- One who recovers from sickness forgets about God.

- A bad son "*bor-bor*" gives his mother "*mama*" a bad name.

- You can hate the watchdog, but do not tell the dog that its teeth "*teet*" are dirty.

- The river that forgets its source will surely dry up.

- A baby "*pickin*" on her mother's "*mama*" back doesn't know that the journey is long.

- A new broom sweeps clean, but an old broom knows the corne*rs*.

Unresolved

- When Joki's wooden stall "*bander*" was burning, I was not around. Why should I put out the fire?

- Do not try to fix a thing when it is not broken.

Unsuccessful, Unproductive, Fruitless, Failed, Disastrous

- If a frog "*uporlor*" is without a tail during its youth, will it take a miracle for it to acquire a tail at old age?

Untrustworthy

- A friend to everybody is a friend to nobody.

- A lie spoils a thousand truths.

- It is when you don't know someone, you call him, you!

- Those that live by the sword will die by the sword.

- As you make your bed, so must you lie on it.

- Lying will get you a wife "*wef*," but it won't keep her.

- Confiding a secret to an unworthy person is like carrying grain in a bag with a hole.

- A fisherman never says his fish stink.

- A man who lies is quick to get married.

- A liar needs a good memory.

- One lie ruins a thousand truths.

- When you are feeding a child "*pickin*," you have to taste the food with your fingers.

- A deceitful woman will place a mortar and a pestle "*martar odoe en martar pensul*" behind the door should her husband knock.

- The truth is difficult to say if it will break up a relationship between husband and wife.

Unwise

- Only a fool tests the depth of water with both feet.

Useless, Hopeless, A Waste of Time

- He took his own foot to lash out his blessings.

- You do not tell the deaf man that there is a commotion in the market square.

Useless but Useful

- All dirty water puts out a fire.

Vacant, Unfilled, Empty

- A woman without a man is like a field without a seed.

Welfare, Interests, Well-Being, Benefit, Good, Happiness, Safety

- It takes the support and effort of an African village to bring up a good child.

Wisdom, Knowledge, Good Judgment, Perception, Intelligence, Understanding, Insight

- A penny saved is a penny gained.

- A minnow does not swim in the same depth of water as the bonita.

- Cut your coat according to your skirt.

- A dog is an effective constable, but it will not patrol the street where the leopard lives.

- When a tricky man dies, a tricky man usually buries him.

- It is when a leopard "*lepet*" is wet that any animal will play around.

- A goat will kick a leopard "*lepet*" when the leopard "*lepet*" is suffering from rheumatism/arthritis.

- A sensible person laughs while abused, but a fool is vexed and retaliates.

- If you do not want the monkey's tail to touch you, do not join the monkey's dance.

- The shoe knows if the stocking has a hole.

- You are seeing the skin of the potato because you are really full.

- If you watch your pot, your food will not burn.

- The gum understands the tooth's affairs.

- A wise man who knows proverbs can reconcile difficulties.

- Wisdom does not come overnight.

- Wisdom is what's left over after we have smartened up.

- Be humble to gain wisdom.

- Knowledge is better than riches.

- He who walks with wise men will be wise.

- Old age does not come in just one day.

Withstand, Endure, Bear Up. Hold Up, Hold Out, Survive
- A woman is born with the ability to achieve success in all areas of her life.

Woman, Lady, Female
- Who doesn't like chattering "*talk talk*" women must stay a bachelor.

- He who marries a beautiful woman marries trouble.

- There is nothing that dries as fast as a woman's tears.

- Do not mix wine with women.

- The mouth of a woman takes no holiday.

- A woman's work is never done.

- A home without a woman is like a barn without cattle.

Work, Labor, Determination

- Nothing comes easy.

- Strive very hard to accomplish your goals.

- An empty bag or sack cannot stand up.

- ***Even the back, part of your body will wait to be clothed, but your stomach will never wait to be fed.***

- By trying often, the monkey learns to jump from the tree.

- If you climb up a ladder, you must start at the bottom.

- Work before pleasure.

- Work is the medicine for poverty.

- Hard work pays off. *"Kill babu to show monkey."*

- All play and no work, does not work.

Worry, Concern, Anxiety, Be Anxious

- Thought breaks the heart.

- If the heart is sad, tears flow.

- Absence makes the heart grows fonder.

- The heart is not a piece of bone.

- Absence makes the heart forget.

- The heart of the wise man lies quiet like clear water.

- When the heart overflows, it comes out through the mouth.

- The heart of a fool is in his mouth, but the mouth of a wise man is in his heart.

- Whatever the ears do not hear, the heart will not sweat or be troubled.

- What comes from the heart goes to the heart.

- The teeth are smiling, but is the heart?

www.ingramcontent.com/pod-product-compliance
Lightning Source LLC
Chambersburg PA
CBHW030411290526
45785CB00004B/1966

* 9 7 8 1 4 5 2 0 1 2 9 2 6 *